MY DYSLEXIA

MY DYSLEXIA

PHILIP SCHULTZ

W. W. NORTON & COMPANY

New York • London

Excerpt from "Stopping by Woods on a Snowy Evening" from the book *The Poetry of Robert Frost*, edited by Edward Connery Lathem. Copyright 1923, 1969 by Henry Holt and Company. Copyright 1951 by Robert Frost. Reprinted by permission of Henry Holt and Company, LLC. "Disintegration" from *The Holy Worm of Praise* by Philip Schultz. Copyright © 2001 by Philip Schultz. Used by permission of Houghton Mifflin Harcourt Publishing Company. All rights reserved. "Balance" and excerpt from "The Magic Kingdom" from *The God of Loneliness* by Philip Schultz. Copyright © 2001 by Philip Schultz. Used by permission of Houghton Mifflin Harcourt Publishing Company. All rights reserved. From *Open Closed Open: Poems* by Yehuda Amichai, translated from the Hebrew by Chana Bloch and Chana Kronfeld. Copyright © 2000 by Chana Bloch and Chana Kronfeld. Used by permission of Houghton Mifflin Harcourt. All rights reserved.

For information about permission to reproduce selections from this book,
write to Permissions, W. W. Norton & Company, Inc.,
500 Fifth Avenue, New York, NY 10110

For information about special discounts for bulk purchases, please contact
W. W. Norton Special Sales at specialsales@wwnorton.com or 800-233-4830

Manufacturing by Courier Westford
Book design by JAM design
Production manager: Julia Druskin

Library of Congress Cataloging-in-Publication Data

Schultz, Philip.
My dyslexia / Philip Schultz. — 1st ed.
p. cm.
ISBN 978-0-393-07964-7 (hardcover)
1. Schultz, Philip. 2. Poets, American—20th century—Biography.
3. Poets, American—21st century—Biography.
4. Dyslexics—United States—Biography. I. Title.
PS3569.C5533Z46 2011
811'.54—dc22
[B]

2011015859

ISBN 978-0-393-34342-7 pbk.

W. W. Norton & Company, Inc.
500 Fifth Avenue, New York, N.Y. 10110
www.wwnorton.com

W. W. Norton & Company Ltd.
Castle House, 75/76 Wells Street, London W1T 3QT

1234567890

For my son Eli,
and his magical, hybrid nature

ACKNOWLEDGMENTS

I would like to thank a number of people who have helped greatly in the writing of this book: first and most of all, my wife, Monica Banks, whose generous support and vast knowledge of this subject provided keen, invaluable insights, without which this book would not have been possible; and my son Eli, whose courage and good humor in the face of adversity has been nothing less than an inspiration to me; as well as my son Augie, who has never failed to make me laugh when laughter was most needed; and especially my fine editor Jill Bialosky, whose idea this book was, and who kept me on course when it seemed impossible; and her assistant Alison Liss, who knows many important things; and my literary agent and friend Georges Borchardt, who is always there; and a number of people whose kind intelligence has meant everything to Eli and me: Carole Symer, Rebecca Di Sunno, Elizabeth Cliff Horowitz, Marty Cooper, Bill O'Hearn, and Paul Weinhold, and all of his many wonderfully supportive teachers and friends. I drew much needed inspiration and guidance from a number of important books about dyslexia, especially Sally Shaywitz's *Overcoming Dyslexia* and Richard Lavoie's *It's So Much Work to Be Your Friend: Helping the Child with Learning Disabilities Find Social Success.* And I would like to call special attention to the remarkable work Jane Ross has been doing for a very long time with her far-reaching and visionary organization Smart Kids with Learning Disabilities; the International Dyslexia Association, a source of invaluable information and support; the Yale Center for Dyslexia and Creativity, an extraordinary source for inspiration and authoritative cutting-edge information on all aspects of dyslexia; and Glenn Corwin, the principal of the groundbreaking Churchill School in Manhattan, where it all started.

Suffering is the substance of life and the root of personality, for it is only suffering that makes us persons.

—MIGUEL DE UNAMUNO

MY DYSLEXIA

I

THE IDEA FOR THIS BOOK CAME OUT OF A COMMENCE-
ment address I gave at the Churchill School in Manhattan,
a high school for the learning disabled, in the spring of
2009. I was given this honor not because I had won the
Pulitzer Prize in poetry the previous spring for my book
Failure, but because I had won it despite the fact that, like
so many of the Churchill School's students, I am dyslexic.
In several interviews I spoke openly about my difficulties in learning to read and the problems it has continued
to pose. I mentioned the fact that I didn't discover I had
dyslexia until I was fifty-eight years old, when my oldest
son was diagnosed with it in the second grade. I learned
from his neuropsychologist's report that we shared many
of the same symptoms, like delayed processing problems,
terrible handwriting, misnaming items, low frustration

tolerance for reading and most homework assignments involving writing, to name a few. Before long I was being asked about my dyslexia in every interview, the first question often being: How did someone who didn't learn to read until he was eleven years old and in the fifth grade, who was held back in third grade and asked to leave his school, come to be a professional poet?

It's a good enough question, but perhaps an ever better one is why I even mention my dyslexia in these interviews. Most of the poems in my book *Failure* concern my father's many business failures and their effect on my mother and me. There's nothing in the book that touches on my dyslexia or my failures as a student. So why had I been so willing, if not eager, to discuss something with strangers that I hadn't discussed at length with my wife or close friends? Even after I found out that I was dyslexic it was my son's problems that concerned me; why did such a bright, sweet-natured boy hate school? How it affected my present life wasn't something I even thought about. But suddenly it seemed to be the only thing I wanted to think about; as if it were a mystery I'd been grappling with my entire life.

It has turned out to be just that: a mystery that had been waiting a long time for me to pay attention to it. And having found its moment it wasn't letting go. But it wasn't a subject I wanted to spend a lot of time thinking about, not when there were so many other more pleasant things to consider. My career, for one thing; it hadn't exactly been thriving before now and suddenly there was an interest in me and my work. Why would I want to revisit all that angst concerning my inability to read, and now, of all times? I decided to stop mentioning it during interviews, even when asked. But it was too late. I was being called by dyslexia organizations, my friends were asking questions, and even my son wanted to know more about my dyslexia. Suddenly everyone I knew it seemed had either suffered from some kind of learning disability or knew someone who did. And I mean everyone. The parents of my younger son's friends told me about their and their children's issues with it in the school parking lot, people waiting for me to sign their copy of my book after one of my readings would talk at length about their own ordeals with learning to read and the long-term effects of delayed processing and their various struggles with language skills, while others waited impatiently behind them. Suddenly everyone wanted to talk to me, it seemed. And not about my poetry: it was my dyslexia they were most interested in.

The first night after hearing the good news, I finally

gave up trying to sleep and came downstairs to find my wife, Monica, sitting at the dining room table, looking equally overwhelmed and bewildered. I was sixty-three years old and had enjoyed a fair share of luck with grants, awards, and publications, though never before had anything on this scale happened to me. When she asked me what I thought this would mean to our lives, I was unable to formulate enough clear thought to articulate even the most basic hint of what I was feeling. We live on what our school, the Writers Studio, provides; we live simply. My wife is a gifted sculptor and no one becomes a sculptor or poet because they're terribly concerned about money.

We own a modest though comfortable house in East Hampton which was purchased during a previous recession and added on to as our family grew. In other words: we live the not uncommon lives of working artists who are lucky enough to maintain a lifestyle sufficient to our needs. I should add that I've always thought of myself as blessed; I love what I do, writing poetry, and I equally love the opportunity of teaching the accomplished hardworking and deserving people who attend my school, and though I often hear myself complaining about being exhausted—and sometimes retell a joke about how my accountant and I finally reached a compromise about my age of retirement: he suggesting ten years after my death and my insisting on only five—I always knew that I had the life I wanted and wouldn't change places with anyone.

So it's little wonder that my wife and I were staring at each other across a table in the middle of a spring night, made anxious by the prospects of possible change—how would things change? More readings, I assumed, knowing that even one or two would amount to more than what I was presently giving, my next collection would most certainly be published now (it hadn't always been a certainty, given the sales of my earlier collections), and my work would most likely be better known, for a while at least—all good things certainly. But then why wasn't I feeling overjoyed?

At first, I was too busy to even try and understand the true meaning of what was happening to me. I've always managed to suffer my rewards with a style of bold incredulity and surprised humility. But now everything seemed different. People expected me to be happy. They expected me to behave in a manner appropriate to the recognition and honor I was being given—they clearly didn't want to hear any complaints or anecdotes about personal conflicts. It wasn't until the following spring, when I gave my talk at the Churchill School, that I began to understand that what I was really feeling during this time was more complicated than a neurotically delayed reaction to good news, that it was something far more personal and byzantine.

I was suffering the mysterious, perplexing, and previously unacknowledged manner in which I received and absorbed all information of any import. I was suffering, to a noticeable degree, by the very manner in which my mind received and then attempted to process information—I was becoming conscious of the convoluted way my mind worked.

AFTER GIVING MY TEN-MINUTE TALK AT CHURCHILL, I was asked to stand onstage in a receiving line for the graduating students. I stood beside the officials of the school, last in line, waiting for this part of the ceremony to begin, and be over with. I felt awkward and anxious. I didn't know these students, had never done anything helpful for them, certainly not in the way their teachers and administrators had. I'd just spoken a few personal words about how I had been affected by my dyslexia—remembering what it felt like to not know why I performed so poorly in school and be held back in third grade and asked to leave the school—I was never even officially diagnosed, and wasn't official, as they were. I looked down at the rows of their bright shining faces, wishing I'd never agreed to speak to them. Having known what they were struggling with, I imagined they'd suffered more, because they were at a school for learning disabled students. There was nothing I said that they didn't already know. And now they would have to smile at me and shake my hand. Now they would have to participate in the charade of acknowledging our bond. Instead of feeling honored, I felt ashamed.

It was a warm June day and I stood there, sweating, wishing someone would turn on the air-conditioning. I could see Monica and my sons looking up at me, perhaps equally embarrassed and uncomfortable. And as the students' names were called I watched each stand and walk up to the stage, taking hold of their diplomas, and then be hugged by the headmaster, the president, and the head of the parents' association. I wasn't prepared for the emotion of this event, for the force of inclusiveness contained in the presentation of the diploma to each student was something more than a seal of personal accomplishment—it was a badge of courage and nobility. The look of surprise and gratitude on their young faces said what they themselves couldn't say: that they understood the enormity of their individual accomplishment, and everyone gathered around them also knew.

When the first young woman graduate approached me I put my hand out, and she smiled and took it warmly. The first two or three students smiled and shook my hand, perhaps somewhat awkwardly. Then a young man, ignoring my outstretched hand, embraced me. He whispered in my ear, "You're part of our family now, I'll never forget what you said, thank you so much." And then I was being embraced and thanked by each graduate. Never before had the difference between the way I felt about myself and the way I was actually being perceived been so apparent, obvious, and unavoidable. Only a few moments before I'd felt like the kid placed in what the other kids called the Dummy Class, someone too dumb to learn to read, or learn anything. And now all these students who'd mastered their great problems so successfully actually wanted to be acknowledged by me?

Standing there, I felt an intense connection to these young fellow travelers. I finally understood why I'd so fervently wanted to talk about my dyslexia during those interviews. I was finally beginning to struggle with those old self-images of myself as someone who didn't belong among the honored. Perhaps I was someone whom others could admire, someone more than a permanent member of the Dummy Class?

2

THIS MUCH IS CLEAR: THE MIND OF A DYSLEXIC IS different from the minds of other people. Learning that my problem with processing language wasn't stupidity seemed to take most of my life. Like every other important trade-off in life, giving up this negative image of myself has been complicated and difficult. I'd grown accustomed to seeing myself as someone who, if fallible and unworthy, had nevertheless managed to do one thing well enough to get recognition for it. I'd learned to accommodate and live around my compromised self in a somewhat comfortable and acceptable manner. Since I was ten I'd taught myself to live a life of opposites— because I couldn't do *this* I learned to enjoy doing *that,* a compensatory way of swimming against constantly shifting currents. It worked well enough: I was happily married, had two terrific boys, a career as a writer, and a private school—which, I would soon come to understand, had been created out of the very thinking process I used to compensate for my dyslexia—all accomplishments of which I was very proud.

A year before I spoke at the Churchill School I was asked to give the commencement address at my son's middle school graduation. At the time I had no idea why I felt compelled to address my dislexia to the thirteen-year-olds heading toward the adolescent rapids of high school, but address it I did. And then, after I'd finished speaking, the father of one of those eighth graders asked me if I'd overcome my difficulties with reading to the point of enjoying it. It was quite a question. Although I'd never really thought about it before, I smiled and said no, I still found reading difficult. Indeed, after living the life of a professional all these years, I still didn't particularly enjoy the actual process of reading.

I love books, especially the ones I own and have collected the way my sons collect baseball cards and kudos for their academic and athletic successes. There's little I enjoy more than sitting on the olive sofa in my study looking around at my books, trying to remember when and where I first read each one and under what circumstances, as if they were photos of old friends. I love the smell and gentle heft and romance of arranging each in its proper and respective place on my shelves. I love most of all the gathering of these very personal and private views of the world I'm being invited to share; the unexpected trust and ever-growing bond and fondness I feel for their authors. Indeed, I love everything about books, except actually reading them.

The act of translating what for me are the mysterious symbols of communication into actual comprehension has always been a hardship to me. I often read a sentence two or three times before I truly understand it; must restructure its syntax and sound out its syllables before I can begin to absorb its meaning and move on to the next sentence. And when I make the mistake of becoming aware that I am reading, and behaving in a way that enables this mysterious, electrically charged process to take place, my mind balks and goes blank and I become anxious and stop.

For reasons I'll never fully understand, or perhaps don't even want to, I dislike the peculiar, obstinate, slightly-out-of-control way in which my mind behaves when I'm reading. I can never just sit down and begin reading, I must first trick myself into it by playing endless games of solitaire on my computer, or reheating my tea or taking another walk with my dog, Penelope, who always seems to know from the odd noises I make that this one activity may soon lead to the other that so pleases her.

But once I'm actually reading, once I've convinced myself that it's in my best interest to engage in this struggle, I proceed haltingly at first, hesitating at the beginning of each new thought and sentence, as if accruing additional strength and courage. And while reading I must sell myself a bill of goods, convince myself that what I'm reading is so fascinating and valuable, so compelling that it's worth the effort. I must remind myself at regular intervals that having to constantly reread sentences is both sensible and necessary, an act of self-discipline, fortitude, and concentration that ultimately will benefit me not only as a person, but as a writer. This argument, and it is an argument, isn't always easy to buy into and sometimes I quit out of frustration and exhaustion. My son's verbal comprehension was scored in the 99.6th percentile on the Wechsler Intelligence Scale, where he demonstrated an "exceptional facility in coming up with category names . . . and an extraordinary rich fund of words," and I would imagine that I share this facility, which helps me compensate for the problems I have with word retrieval and identifying common concepts. I often forget the meaning of words I've looked up many times before and must consult a dictionary as I frequently consult a thesaurus while writing to make sure I've selected the right word. As I read, a kind of subtle bartering between uncertainty and hunger for knowledge goes on in my mind, in which I must conquer a feeling of hopelessness and anxiety. I've learned to read the way a runner learns to expect and find his second and third winds, the way an athlete pushes himself beyond where it is comfortable to go. I read word by word, sometimes congratulating myself on the completion of each sentence, each paragraph and chapter. Perhaps this is why it's particularly hard for me to read anything that isn't well written and moving; why I became a poet, because poetry is so compressed and is often beautifully written and moving.

All of which, without doubt, makes the fact of my being a writer even more strange, and, to a degree, wonderfully preposterous.

I remember the first time I even considered the idea of being a writer. I was in the fifth grade when my reading tutor, whom I had been forced to see after my parents were threatened with the possibility of yet another expulsion (my birthday being in January, I'd started kindergarten a year early and in a school out of my neighborhood and I was held back and asked to leave the school when my behavior became a problem) asked me out of the blue what I thought I might like to do with my life.

Without a moment's hesitation, I answered that I wanted to be a writer.

My reading tutor was a retired grade school principal, a good-natured, slightly stern man who was so overweight the opening in his desk couldn't accommodate the width of his belly and he sat so far away from it he couldn't easily reach anything on his desktop. When he laughed his belly moved in gelatinous waves all the way from his chin down to his knees. And now he was laughing, really laughing. What was so funny about a boy who couldn't read at the age of eleven saying he wanted to become someone who spends most of his time doing precisely that? The fact that I couldn't read didn't mean that I never would, I thought. I always assumed I would one day, and what difference would it then make? But Mr. Joyce—and only many years later did I appreciate the irony of his name—couldn't stop laughing. He kept wiping the tears from his eyes, apologizing, and then starting up again, laughing even harder this time.

"Philip, my dear boy, why in the world do you imagine

you want to do something for the rest of your life that has been so hard for you to do on its most basic level?" he asked, holding his belly as if to control further eruptions.

I could only manage a small shrug. I had absolutely no idea why. And I wasn't insulted, I was just curious.

"How long have you wanted to be a writer?"

"Not very long," I ventured.

"How long then?"

"Since you asked me. I never thought about it before."

Now he started laughing again, with even greater force and enthusiasm.

Later that night, in bed, after I told my mother what I'd told Mr. Joyce and we were reading my Blackhawk comic books together—she would read the words aloud and I would imitate the sounds, as if reading them myself—I surprised both of us by interrupting her and actually reading the words. I remember the way she sat there, staring at me, her eyes wide as I read without pausing for breath, afraid if I stopped I would never be able to begin again. I sang each word, smiling, looking over her shoulder at the January moon, which I could see through my torn window shade, big and gaunt-looking, smiling down at me, it seemed, as if with wonder. It was the same wonder I felt as I remembered another January day two years earlier when my mother had been called to my previous school by my teacher and the school principal.

<hr />

MY THIRD GRADE TEACHER TOLD MY MOTHER THAT I never followed instructions, paid attention, or obeyed the simplest directions. I left class when I pleased and got into fights with other boys, the principal told her. I'd rubbed a boy's face against a cement culvert in the playground the day before, cutting his cheek and mouth. What they didn't tell her is what this boy, along with other boys, had said to me to make me so angry: he said I was a dummy who couldn't learn anything. So I did what I saw my father and my uncle do when someone insulted them, what all the tough guys in all the movies and on TV did when insulted—I hit kids, with all my strength, to make them stop laughing at me.

The principal told my mother that he saw no other recourse than to expel me from school. As he spoke my mother's eyes grew small and hard. She was trying not to cry, I thought, because she didn't want him to see how much this was hurting her. But why didn't they tell her what those kids had done? They had mimicked my stuttering—why weren't their mothers called to school? He looked and spoke only to her, as if I weren't there, standing next to her, as if I were invisible. It was the way I felt in school, listening to the teacher talk only to the other children, as if she didn't think I would understand what she was saying, as if it was a waste of time talking to me. Since I couldn't be expected to begin my next school at the fourth grade, the principal added, I was being held back a year. The school I would attend when I finished fourth grade was called the Number Nine School. My mother knew it was the worst school in Rochester, a place famous for the number of kids who left it to attend reformatory.

It was snowing as we walked home but my mother didn't seem to notice the snow, or that I was hurrying to keep up with her. She always held my hand, but not now. She was walking quickly, as if trying to get away from me. When she slipped on ice and fell into a slush puddle and just sat there, looking up at me, sighing, I wanted to keep on walking.

My mother never lied to me. She'd told me what the

big scar on her belly was, because they had cut her open to pull me out so I could be born. She told me that I didn't have a brother or sister because she had lost a baby girl the year before I was born and her doctor said it was too dangerous for her to give birth again. She wanted me so much she didn't care, she said. Each night while putting me to sleep she'd tell me how much she loved me, that I was the best thing that ever happened to her. And that she wanted me to do well in school because she'd loved going to school, loved learning with all her heart, but that her Polish immigrant father made her leave school to help support their family. She told me how much she hated being uneducated and not knowing things everyone else knew. I would change all that for her, she said. I would do everything she couldn't do. I would make something out of myself. I would make her proud.

And now I was being held back and kicked out of school and going to the worst school in upstate New York. I wasn't the one thing in her life that she'd done right.

She sat there, in the wet snow, looking up at me.

Anything was better than seeing her this way, I thought. Anything.

AND NOW I WAS READING. AND MY MOTHER WAS smiling at me.

"Philip," she said, "you're reading, all by yourself!"

"Yes," I said, "I'm reading!"

"Is it because you told Mr. Joyce you wanted to be a writer and he laughed at you?"

"I didn't care if he laughed."

"But you're reading, Philip. Like you always knew how."

Yes, I thought, like I always really knew how.

And if you can read you can write, I thought to myself.

It was that simple.

3

THERE'S ONE ESSENTIAL THING I NOW UNDERSTAND
about my dyslexia: that writing a book about it also means
writing one about my anxiety. Coping with anxiety, and
avoiding it, has become a way of life for me. When I was
in school little was known about medical interventions or
cognitive behavioral therapy; if anyone was talking about
serotonin levels or "derailing the negative thought patterns," it certainly didn't make its way to where I lived.
Everything seemed to boil down to my "nervousness."

I sometimes deliberately take the wrong direction
while driving because, in my roundabout way of thinking, the most direct route sometimes involves making
decisions my mind doesn't like making. A simple thing
like turning right instead of left can become a game of
strategy in which the goal is mastering a baffling world

of logic that has nothing to do with winning or losing, or self-esteem. I wish I could call this magical thinking but it's more like Talmudic thinking in the sense that every decision or idea attracts a horde of fierce self-commentaries which automatically refer to a vast switchboard of do's and don'ts, reasons and anti-reasons, all of which reside within the subcontinent of each decision I make, no matter how innocent, wholesome, munificent, or mundane.

In other words, the wrong way is the right way, once you consider the quirky hard angles and dangerous curves along this devious highway. This may sound like a somewhat idealized form of paranoia, but it's nothing that esoteric, or commonplace. It's simply a business-as-usual way of passing muster within the confines of a dizzyingly strict sense of urgency that approaches life from all sides at once, a furtive second-guessing and metaphysical one-upmanship in which my mind must always keep a step ahead of itself, and everything else. My mind plans responses to actions that haven't as yet been put into action or, in many cases, even imagined. This has nothing to do with the art of living, and everything to do with intrigue and preparation for further struggle. It goes without saying that I'm good at chess. Thinking one or two steps ahead comes naturally to me. This way of thinking I now understand comes from compensating for my dyslexia.

I understood that I was different from other kids. I lived in a world of differences measured not by appearances, wealth, or even intelligence. The world I lived in involved struggle for control over my thoughts and actions. My differentness felt freakish. My brain wouldn't obey me, nor my parents or my teachers. If I had trouble learning to read a clock, know my left from my right, hearing instructions—things everyone else seem to do easily—how could I trust my own thoughts or anything about myself? Everything a teacher said would make me angry and distracted; if I thought I was being asked to do something she already knew I couldn't do, I would feel attacked and cornered. I hated rules and tests of all kinds. I almost never understood what was being asked of me, and I almost always suspected its motives.

Everything that frightened me made me anxious— the more fearful I grew, the more anxious I became— and almost everything seemed to make me anxious. For instance, my wife knows better than to startle me by appearing suddenly, especially if I'm writing or trying to read; in order to concentrate I have to envelop myself in a cocoon of privacy carefully constructed out of silence and self-will. My mind doesn't like reading, spelling, making sense of recipes, maps, hearing directions or instructions of any kind, making any kind of split-second decision, or paying attention to an entire conversation. For a very long time I believed that every answering machine I ever owned never recorded a telephone number correctly. I would have to ask people to repeat things several times before I managed to hear them because I told myself I was somewhat hard of hearing (which I still prefer to believe on occasion). Anything whispered, insinuated, or abbreviated becomes in my mind a mumble-jumble of bargain-basement gibberish. It was astonishing to finally realize that my difficulties were part of a larger problem that wasn't my fault alone, but my brain's, that there was a scientific modus operandi behind everything I'd come to see as the peculiarities of a besieged personality. It was amazing to comprehend that all the cat-and-mouse games my mind plays, all its endless scheming and compensatory, roundabout thinking, not only owned a name, but was a disability many others also suffered from, in many cases knowingly. My son has known what has troubled him since he was seven years old, knowing he's dyslexic helps him to understand why certain things are more difficult for him. It's comforting for him knowing he can have extra time to take tests and be in a quiet, peaceful place, somewhat free of pressure and stress, and that he's as smart as the smartest kids in his class. That the trouble his mind causes him isn't really his fault; that it isn't a matter of blame, or shame.

Now I knew why I was always well past my desired exit by the time I understood a tollbooth operator's direction, shouted at our GPS: "Left?—which left goddamnit!?"—couldn't under any circumstance introduce people and get their names right and called my sons each by the other's name, sometimes merging them into Augie-Eli or Eli-Augie. Why I could never take lecture notes or read my own handwriting, drifted around the bend of nearly every conversation, which I heard only in pieces and which often feel like riddles or puzzles I'd have to later restructure and decode; why all those years of psychotherapy left so much unexplained and, finally, why I became a teacher, someone who does all the talking. Now I understood why I felt truly comfortable and safe only when I was alone, with no one asking anything of me that I couldn't do. Why, to this day, I bite my nails, pick at myself, and jump at loud noises, sigh constantly, and go blank when confronted with other people's expectations. And why, when starting this book, I became depressed and couldn't write for months, couldn't even think about my subject without wanting to flee a crime scene. I'm not by nature a depressive; in the past my depressions were always brief and usually linked with romantic failures, bouts of loneliness, and rejections related to my work—the usual psychic entanglements of young writers. But never had I suffered a real depression for very long, and certainly not concerning my work. And now even thinking about writing about my dyslexia depressed me.

Then one cold March morning I took an early morning walk on the beach with my wife and our dog, Penelope, an act that almost always clears my head. It is without doubt one of the real benefits of living in East Hampton, where we're surrounded by the ocean and bays along the Long Island Sound. The beach is where I usually get my best ideas. And on this particular morning the ocean looked immaculate and welcoming, the great roiling waves breaking along the shoreline with a forthrightness both all-encompassing and inspiringly deliberate. Trying to read the alliterative language of the waves, tokens of foment and constant agitation, my anxiety—which for so long seemed a sovereign government, ubiquitous, and secretive—now was being called into question. What, I asked my wife, was making me so depressed? My book,

Monica said. Yes, of course it was my book—irritability and contrariness are sister demons of all depressions. But what exactly about my being dyslexic was so terrifying?

And then I realized it was my anxiety! Looking back was making me so anxious my mind was defending itself by depressing my thoughts. I was able to write that very day and the day after that. My depression was gone.

It's a tricky business, trying to understand the labyrinthine and subterranean circuitry of one's own mind, tricky but also necessary for someone for whom thought itself must often be translated, interpreted, and censored before being transmitted. Part of me has always lived in fear of the way my mind thinks, and behaves, as if it weren't entirely in my control, or belonged to someone who wasn't always sympathetic to me. It's a fear as old and helpless as my earliest perception of myself. For this reason perhaps I remember the movie house where I first saw Stanley Kubrick's *2001: A Space Odyssey,* the seat and row I sat in, how old I was (a Thursday afternoon two days before my twenty-fourth birthday, the Golden Gate Theatre in San Francisco). I remember clearly being terrified when the spaceship's computer, Hal, attacked the astronauts. The movie seemed to be addressing my precarious relationship with my own brain, which so often left me feeling ridiculously expansive and indefinite, excited and vulnerable at the same time. The astronauts had become dependent on Hal, and took him for granted. He was their brain, the central governing system that ran the spaceship and organized their lives. And suddenly, in order to survive, they had to realize Hal was also their enemy, that he meant them harm. I felt this way when I realized that my brain was using anxiety to control what I could understand, and write about, that it was trying to censor my thoughts. My struggle with depression and anxiety goes back to the time when I first tried to learn to read, and probably before that. Kubrick seemed to be telling me that my mind had its own agenda, that, given the right circumstance, it was possible that one's own intelligence could be used against us, to the point of obsolescence and self-extinction. The moment when the surviving astronaut finally manages to disconnect Hal and regain control of his spaceship was triumphant for me. I found myself in tears, utterly confused. I remember each of the five miles I walked across town back to my small apartment in Noe Valley, the amazing silence of my wonderment. What I'd always suspected was true: my mind couldn't be trusted; it was a potential enemy.

4

I COULD CLAIM THAT I INVENTED MYSELF OUT OF the many things I couldn't do so I could do one or two things well enough to win the self-respect and admiration I desired so fervently. I could claim a great many things, but the truth has more to do with the way my brain was, and is, neurologically wired. In a sense, it's wired for loneliness. It excludes others by its very nature of differentness, its patina of abnormality. This is an especially important issue for children, for whom anything abnormal is frightening and off-putting. And my behavior was always unusual.

On my first day of kindergarten my mother left me suddenly without first preparing me to be left alone, and without even saying goodbye. Probably fearing I'd make a scene, she dropped my hand and hurried out the door. Alone, surrounded by strangers, I climbed up on a table and started screaming. There's a fancy phrase for this—separation anxiety—but it doesn't come close to describing the terror I felt. My mother may have tried to explain why she had to leave but it no longer made any difference: I was screaming and no one—not the teachers, staff, nor school psychologist—could calm me down. My mother had to remain in class with me when I returned to school days later, the way she had to sleep with me before I could be alone in the dark. I always believed this fear of the dark was a manifestation of my being an only child enclosed in a world made of the disappointments and egocentricities of the people around me, and to some extent, that's probably true. But now I know it was more than that. It was my anxiety about being different, most likely related to my dyslexia, that fostered this fear.

I think of the line by Marianne Moore from her essay "If I Were Sixteen Today": "The cure for loneliness is solitude." Yes, indeed, how apt, and concise. This wonderfully wise poet understood the important distinction between the two. Loneliness is a state of longing and incompleteness, which causes pain and depression, and in extreme cases can be deadly. Solitude is a choice, a preference necessary to making art and thought. The trick for me was in learning to tolerate loneliness as a necessary and natural state of being, even though it left me feeling entrenched and painfully unaligned. The truth is I preferred loneliness to my fear of my father's and uncle Jake's violent rages. My friends were imaginary personages who offered solace and remediation and resided entirely in my personal mythology. To this day, after a reading, having shared intimate details of my life with strangers, I want to be alone, and given the opportunity, I will escape through a back door to spend a few moments alone on a stairway or in a parking lot, enjoying the solitude and quiet, away from the expectation of others. Unable to sleep, I'll often sit in the dark of my dining room, sipping vodka out of a shot glass, my sons upstairs, turning in their sleep, my wife two rooms away in the comfort of our bed, Penelope curled at my feet. These few moments of solitude are a state of truce, a no-man's-land between belonging somewhere, finally, and nowhere at all.

DURING MY LAST YEAR AT THE SCHOOL I WAS ASKED to leave, I ate my lunches alone in a nearby Hungarian family-style restaurant filled with men and women from Bond's, Hickey Freeman, and Fashion Park men's clothing factories in Rochester. My mother didn't know I was stealing coins from my father's vending machines and throwing her lunches away on my way to school. She thought I was eating in the school cafeteria with all the other kids. For certain she didn't know that none of them wanted to sit with me, or that they made fun of me even when I sat by myself at a table across the room. Richard Lavoie's *It's So Much Work to Be Your Friend* addresses in brilliant detail the difficulty kids with learning disabilities have making and keeping friends; how having few social skills makes them behave in a way that pushes other kids away. I thought not being able to learn anything made everyone hate me. I had no idea that my dyslexia was the reason I ate alone every day in a restaurant with blue and red unicorns on the wallpaper, ordering the same dish of Hungarian goulash and a glass of milk, even though I detested milk almost as much as the sticky, always too hot stew of dark meat and overcooked potatoes and vegetables. I ordered the same thing every day because I'd overheard a man ordering it on my first afternoon there and I couldn't read the menu and was too embarrassed to ask the waitress.

I will never forget the sad, tired faces of the men eating silently at the counter, reading their newspapers before returning to the kind of jobs my mother said I would have if I didn't learn to read and write. I watched as they chewed, frowning like robots. The white-haired waitress always asked if there wasn't something else she could get me, since I hardly ever touched my food. But I preferred being alone to the terror of the school cafeteria. This tiny restaurant was in the midst of the men's clothing industry in Rochester—an industry where both my grandfathers came to work as tailors, Jewish immigrants going either to New York City to work in the women's garment center or to Rochester in the men's—with its tiny refugee army of men and women. My mother worked as a filing clerk until she was thirty-three and married my father. It was low-paid repetitive work she hated with every fiber of her being, and she couldn't bear to think her only child might have to do it as well. Why had she suffered all that if not for me—to ensure that my life would be infinitely more rewarding than hers?

The languages my grandma and her friends spoke were as broken and insufficient as the fences, shingles, and roofs of our neighborhood, where everyone was always too tired to fix anything. And now my mind was broken, too.

What I remember best about those long lonely afternoons in Rochester is the corner table with the plastic red-checkered tablecloth where I sat looking out the window at the endlessly falling snow. What did it matter if I kept losing my temper or couldn't organize my thoughts into understandable patterns of speech; if I thought multiplication tables meant "many tables" and got scared every time a teacher looked my way; if I couldn't add and subtract, spell or know who the president of the United States was; if I was the stupidest kid in the world? In those few moments, staring out that window at the endless snow, all that mattered was that no one, not even myself, seemed to be holding me in disfavor, judging me as unworthy of respect and affection. All that mattered was this respite of peaceful nothingness, which I loved beyond reproach.

5

"NO ONE UNDERSTOOD," MAXIM GORKY DECLARED, "so clearly as Anton Chekhov the tragic element in life's trivialities." Indeed, no one understood so clearly the trivial lives of peasants as Chekhov, who said in his short story of that name: "Yes, it was terrible living with these people . . . there was nothing in their lives that did not provide . . . killing work . . . without any help and nowhere to find it . . . ." It wasn't exactly Chekhov's nineteenth-century Russia out my bedroom window, but I did hear stories from my parents, relatives, and our neighbors about life in Russia, Poland, and Lithuania, about ghettos, shtetls, and living fretfully, without rights or reason to hope for change. No one on Maria Street in the 1950s knew there was even the possibility of change, and hope wasn't what many of us felt entitled to. Our inheritance was a poverty of expansiveness, of the peasant soul itself. Mine was a family, a neighborhood of peasant suffering, envy and submissiveness, fear and suspicion. Everyone hoarded grudges, stared suspiciously at everyone else, angrily looked down at others one rung lower down the ladder of unworthiness. My mind even looked down on itself, always apologizing and making excuses for what it couldn't do, perform, or understand. Immigrant and peasant logic, like dyslexic thinking, is a strategy for survival.

Dyslexia invokes scorn and repulsion from even those suffering it. A temple of disorganization, insufficiency, and obdurate servitude, it's a syndrome of endless apology and explanation. To overcome it one must engage in "killing work and ache all over at night without any help and nowhere to find it"—this is the way Chekhov describes the peasant life in the same story. Even with modern science and technology, every dyslexic must forge his own "strategy for survival." The students at the Churchill School enjoyed and benefited from trained, caring teachers and specialized courses, but they were essentially on their own, and knew it. They knew through experience that they had to learn to compensate for their inability to immediately process written and spoken language and that regardless of the quality and sensitivity of the education they receive, they have to learn how to adapt independently to each difficult situation. All the help and support in the world doesn't alleviate the stress of trying to read a recipe or manual or learn a foreign language; doesn't mitigate the burden of loneliness. Emerson said it best perhaps: "For nonconformity the world whips you with its displeasure." And dyslexia is nothing if not nonconformity, the very essence of being different and apart. Dyslexia is a disability that pleads for pardon and forgiveness, that creates its own alternate logic, a world unto itself.

I never meant to be annoying, forgetful, delayed, overwhelmed, and dumb-sounding and -looking. I never wanted to be made fun of or anger my teachers or keep an entire class late because I didn't understand a concept. But that's what often happened as a consequence of my learning disability.

I don't pretend to understand why I got into so much trouble during my first weeks at my new school—where I had to repeat third grade—especially since trouble was the one thing I wanted to avoid. It was probably a mixture of many things I'll never be able to sort through. My dyslexia didn't play a part at first because no one knew that I didn't know how to read or had problems learning things. No one knew what had happened at my previous school.

The trouble began when I was told by two kids my age that I had to pay them my lunch money to go to school. Pay or get beaten up. All the Jewish kids paid, they said. This gang of toughs in the fourth and fifth grades didn't expect a skinny small-for-my-age Jewish kid new to the school to fight back. They certainly didn't expect me not to be afraid of them. But before long I was fighting one or two kids every day after school, worrying that each day there was my last. I didn't want to hurt my mother again, but I wasn't about to fork over my lunch money and I certainly didn't like being picked on because I was Jewish. Once my new teacher asked about my black eyes, cut lips, and swollen face, wondering perhaps if I was being abused at home, but when I said nothing, she just nodded and walked away. I quickly discovered that was pretty much the end of any concern on the part of the school. Once again, I was on my own.

My mother never seemed to notice my condition when I came home. I was fighting bigger, older kids nearly every day in the playground after school, with other kids cheering every time I got walloped. The next morning I'd sit at my desk expecting to get called into the principal's office. Once I was asked by a gym teacher why I was sighing so much. And once a janitor saw me crying in an alcove and asked if I was okay. If anything, most of the kids there seemed to take pleasure in my being bullied. Maybe it was because they were glad it was happening to me instead of them, or they thought my fighting back would make things harder for them. Things got worse until the day my class had to stay after school because of something I did—I was caught by a teacher talking to someone, I think—and suddenly everyone was whispering about "getting me" after school. And that's what happened: every kid in third and fourth grades blocked every exit door so I couldn't get away. I was in the Dummy Class by then but that wasn't why it happened. I was fighting back and making trouble for those who weren't, but that wasn't why either.

I used to view my fighting as a matter of honor, of bravery and cowardice. I was a street kid who followed the rules of the street, which provided me with the only real education and self-respect I knew. These rules served as a buffer against the confusion of my home life and, later, against the anxiety my dyslexia created. Primitive and basic, the laws were well defined and therefore honorable. In this immigrant world of minimum-wage earners, trust and generosity was suspect, affection a liability, and one never snitched on anyone, ever. To this day I can recognize in someone's eyes and bearing a quality I can only call "street." It's evident in the way they refuse to look squarely back at you, the way in which they withhold admiration and affection, a recklessness devoid of expectation and entitlement that owns no faith in there being a common good. No amount of education and success can erase this quality, nor can any amount of therapy or learned rules of speech and etiquette gloss over the controlled disturbances boiling under the surface calm of such a personality. Every street kid I knew shared one belief: that no matter how bad things were outside, what was going on at home was far worse. The rules outside, though ruthless, were clear and one was grateful for it.

I think my choosing to fight had something to do with the manner in which my mind reacted to stress and fear. When I was challenged my mind would go dark; I'd believe I had no recourse, other than to strike back. The other kids were negotiating with the bullies, paying them as a way of avoiding greater trouble. They were using reason and diplomacy as weapons. They understood that it wasn't really necessary to fight to the death over every insult.

Herman Melville powerfully describes this disintegration in *Billy Budd*. After being falsely accused of disloyalty and dereliction of duty, Billy stares haplessly at Captain Vere, his silence intensifying into "a convulsed tongue-tie" and "an agony of ineffectual eagerness to obey the injunction to speak and defend himself." His mind is locked, he fears, permanently in a "struggle against suffocation." Billy can't speak up in his own defense so instead he strikes and kills his tormentor, thus bringing about his court-martial and death by hanging. Billy is a pure and simple soul who can't countenance a charge of disloyalty and subterfuge; his shame is too great to contain. His is an automatic response: failure/panic/disconnection.

The same kind of automatic impulse, or some version of it, goes on in the minds of every dyslexic when confronted with shame and embarrassment. One stands staring into space, unable to do or say anything to defend oneself and respond appropriately, until finally one must do something to release oneself from what seems an unbearable pressure both physical and mental.

Disintegration, I now understand, comes directly out of my dyslexia. It's a reflex in which I can perceive what's happening but feel helpless to do or say anything to exonerate myself. All conscious thought disintegrates. I once wrote a poem describing the sensation:

the way the mind leaves fingerprints on   every memory
    tissue
say: all those dreams auditioning for   infinitesimally minor
    roles   in

insignificant family dramas   walking thin lines   between
    abstract design
& routine delusion   not being whole   but disavowed   as
    in: denuded,

it happens so quickly   one minute your ideas are listening
    & then pain
explodes into chronic babble   slicing the tongue into
    fervent   opinions,

suddenly everything is: twitching   the left side of your
    body is: laughing,
but you feel   nothing   while the body is hysturicall   wit
    juy   forget ieet,

play it no hind,   relux, there are mulch mare specticulair
    events lappening
hang loose Mr Moose   dear sweetcaboose   I'm stuck up
    ta me noose in rust

compost   lust und deluge   onelittlepiggietwoolittlepiggie
   eee ful
like ragin urge   cause ieet huurts   it's allyacando   deer
   Gid

is: scream me fuckin' heedoff   furst thun in da mournin
   duurrlin

I wrote this in the late nineties when I didn't understand I was dyslexic. I was trying to describe the linguistic and phonetic breakdown I experience, using humor
to lighten the terror. I had in mind memories of being
bullied, though I had no idea why I made such a good
target for them. To some extent bullies depend on their
victims feeling helpless and losing all conscious control
of their ability to reason. This is why they so often taunt
in a public arena where the shame and stress is greatest
for their victims. The real shame is that the victims of
bullying, certainly dyslexic ones, don't understand that
the way their mind processes information isn't a matter of
weakness or blame; that their inability to "answer back"
isn't their fault. Athletes use the phrase "muscle memory"
to explain their bodies' ability to respond instinctually
to situations that pose similar challenges. The dyslexic's

mind is a muscle that remembers to protect itself against its memory of painful events. It shuts down when it becomes overloaded in order to spare itself further stress; this happens instantaneously, without warning.

After the beatings, our school's assistant principal came to our house. My mother, fearing the worst, was relieved when the woman asked for the names of the students responsible. I played dumb, of course, and before leaving, she asked about my learning problems at my previous school. Embarrassed, my mother said I was a slow learner. The woman had read my dossier and probably knew it was a lot more than that. My mother's younger brother was an institutionalized schizophrenic. Her older brother Jake hardly ever left his bedroom and constantly fought with everyone—I suspect she didn't want me examined any closer. A stupid, angry kid was better than a crazy one. I can well imagine the disheveled logic and desperation that went into her not seeking help for me, except for the remedial help forced on her by my school. We both suspected the worst. In our black-and-white worlds, brains weren't wired differently, you either were someone to boast about or to be ashamed of.

6

I WAS LEFT ALONE BY THE BULLIES WHEN I RETURNED to school—I found out the reason many years later: my father had had a little talk with the gang leader's father, a drunkard who lived on disability assistance. Back when it mattered it would've meant a great deal to me to know he'd acted on my behalf, but in some ways being scared and fighting was better than being lonely and ignored. Suddenly I was placed in a special class within a class, consisting of a table near the coatroom, and sat with two other kids, staring out large dirty windows overlooking a tar roof of smokestacks, ventilation pipes, and a collection of discarded and broken chairs, desks, and old lunch pails. A good tableau for those deemed lost and discarded. One of the other kids at my table was a new kid to the school, Billy Saunders. He was a skinny runt who bragged he never took guff from anyone and was in more fights than even I was. He'd heard about everyone ganging up on me and thought I deserved a medal of honor for fighting back. The third member of our tiny clique was a girl named Emily who smelled bad and sucked her thumb all day. If I had to venture a guess, I would say she suffered from some form of undiagnosed autism, because she had no ostensible personality and gazed inward. When she looked at me she hummed and tapped her fingers and stared into infinity as if she hadn't seen me. I never once saw her smile. After a while I barely noticed her and came to see her as dumb, the way everyone else saw Billy and me. There were no gradations in dumbness, apparently, just one vast slab of abject grayness.

Not much was known about dyslexia in 1956, certainly not in our particular school in Rochester's inner city. Lack of training and exhaustion forced many of these teachers, already overwhelmed by overcrowding and a range of other frustrations, to segregate the learners from the non-learners. We—the non-learners—were pretty much left to ourselves. I have a memory from that time in which a book was placed in my hands by our teacher. "Here, look at the pictures, just sit there pretending you're reading it," she said. Did she really say this? Would any self-respecting teacher actually say something like this to a child in her class? Having seen all the hard, dedicated work teachers do in my children's classes, and all the truly inspired teachers I've had the pleasure to work with as a visiting poet in third, fourth, fifth, and sixth grade classes in various schools around the country, I find it hard to believe. But the memory persists.

My teachers were most likely performing the best they could under demanding and thankless conditions. Kids like me, Billy, and Emily were expected to fall through the cracks. While addressing the rest of the class, our teacher would turn her back on us as if we weren't worthy of being addressed. It was understood by everyone that we had been given up on. Being given up on is a very peculiar feeling. I'd sit at my desk looking at the shared picture book, pretending not to be eavesdropping on the conversation taking place beyond the assumed reach of my intelligence, staring at the pictures with all the intensity I could muster in order to avoid having to look up into anyone's eyes. Occasionally Billy would kick me under the table, trying to make me laugh. Sometimes I would make a face or pretend to be bored but it was all playacting— I wanted desperately to be included, to be perceived as being presentable enough to be addressed.

But Billy didn't seem to mind being seen this way; in fact, he took it as a compliment. Since it was obvious that we knew things the others didn't—like how to breathe through our ears and make firecrackers out of Drano and Epsom salt—they were the real dummies. He named us after popular TV western stars: he was Poncho the Moron while I was the Cisco Kid Idiot. We invented a secret three-fingered handshake and a way of pronouncing words by half whispering, half swallowing them, a secret guttural language consisting of grunts and whistles for and by morons. We kidded each other about who was more stupid and who had the worst father. His, a toothless, overweight drunken night-shift janitor at DuPont's who lived with someone Billy claimed was a professional prostitute, won hands down. His younger brother Ronnie, who put on shows for us wearing her hats and underwear, claimed he knew more about sex than anyone in the Finger Lakes and proved it by going on to become a cross-dressing teenage prostitute. We spent a good deal of time playing hooky, stealing cans of soup, spaghetti, peaches, and candy bars from Levi's grocery, capturing butterflies in jars and looking at his father's enormous collection of nudists' magazines. I was never sure what Billy liked about me but I admired his fearless tenacity and headlong appetite for adventure and bravado. He was my one friend, the only one I can remember having in grade or high school. His belief in embracing one's position in the world as an honor bestowed upon the chosen and select no matter how low or disposable, is an idea I still hold dear. It was a position and ours. Our friendship, I imagined, was the kind soldiers forged in war, a bond born of survival, familiarity, and mutual respect. His attitude was that our being placed at the Dummy Table was a position and bond of privilege. I was saddened to hear many years later, after I'd left for college, that Billy had joined the army and was killed in Vietnam.

BY THE TIME I GOT TO HIGH SCHOOL I READ WELL enough to pass most of my classes with B's and C's. My father and his brothers were natural storytellers, each always trying to outdo the other at family occasions, so I'd grown up with an appreciation for the art of storytelling and sometimes even enjoyed the short stories and novels I read in my English classes, despite the extra effort I had to make to "hear" the stories over the screen of anxiety the actual process of reading created. I was usually articulate enough to describe what I did read in papers or to my teachers to get passing grades, or even to impress them with my verbal comprehension. I did retain well what I managed to read. I also discovered I had a flair for writing papers in my freshman year, and would spend a good deal of time getting the grammar—never an easy task for me—and syntax of each sentence right. I was always goal-oriented so I worked hard to get passing grades on most of my tests. Because I heard so little of what my teachers said in class I sometimes had to memorize portions of textbooks, and because I processed information so slowly I disliked lectures of any kind. My son's knowing why he encountered such difficulty in his classes has made a large difference to him. My ignorance of my dyslexia only intensified my sense of isolation and hopelessness. Ignorance is perhaps the most painful aspect of a learning disability.

Getting by in classes I didn't like—like science, math, and Latin—was such hard work by the time I got to high school I knew that getting by wasn't going to get me into college. Although much of high school is a blur, as so many things were at the time, I somehow assumed I'd get through high school and go to college, perhaps because the alternative was too painful to consider. Getting away from Rochester and going off on my own were palpable desires by my second year of high school. Anything, even having to read all the time, was better than the life my uncle Jake lived in his tiny room off our kitchen, listening to a police radio and opening and closing curtains at the Paramount, and I certainly didn't want to work in a department store filing papers as my mother did. My father never expressed any interest in my going to college but his endless struggles convinced me that an education was the only real way out for me. My mother would hire neighborhood boys to do my chores so I could study. I remember the feeling of achievement and importance this gave me, knowing that, despite everything, she had faith in me, and believed I would make something of myself.

And somewhere even beyond my mother's confidence was a feeling of self-worth, an inchoate sense of future achievement that allowed me to believe I would get away from this peasant world of endless strife. I managed to read well enough to pass my classes and rewarded myself with art courses I enjoyed. I became the high school cartoonist, and wrote poems and stories for the literary magazine. Each small success built on the previous one and they each made a difference to me. I had few friends and spent most of my time going to movies, drawing, and helping my father with his vending business on the weekends. And then, sometime during my sophomore year in high school, I fell in love with books. Not reading, but books themselves. I didn't understand the distinction at the time, but suddenly—overnight it seemed—I found myself loving to identify with the expansiveness of the narrators' visions of the world—a much larger vision than my own—and with the way their characters struggled to understand their own limitations. My dyslexia was certainly slowing me down, but it wasn't stopping me from using my emotions as a springboard to imagining the larger, richer world these books offered me.

I remember the first book I fell in love with: *The Moviegoer* by Walker Percy. I was fifteen and browsing in a convenience store, waiting for my mother to have her hair done in the shop next door, where she went every Thursday. I can't say why I was with her or what I was doing looking at books in a revolving stand near the cashier counter, but I clearly remember my fascination when I read the citation on the book's back cover. I didn't know what a National Book Award for Fiction was and I can't remember ever picking up a novel on my own before, not outside of what I had to read for my English classes. But I read the citation over and over again:

> *The Moviegoer*, an intimation rather than a statement of mortality and the inevitability of that condition, is a truthful novel with shocks of recognition and spasms of nostalgia for every—or nearly every—American. Mr. Percy, with compassion and without sentimentality or the mannerisms of the clinic, examines the delusions and hallucinations and the daydreams and the dreams that afflict those who abstain from the customary ways of making do.
>
> LEWISH GANNETT, HERBERT GOLD, JEAN STAFFORD, Judges, 1962 National Book Award for Fiction

I have absolutely no idea why I found these words so fascinating, but I did know how much I wanted someone to say such things about me. No doubt the judges' reference to the author as *Mr.* Percy impressed me. Their respect for his accomplishment was so great they didn't use his first name—*Mr.* Percy! I'm certain I didn't know what the phrases "shocks of recognition" and "spasms of nostalgia" or "mannerisms of the clinic" meant, but I was deeply impressed that this writer had written something that could inspire such praise and admiration. I understood that it was good to be "truthful" when writing about serious matters like people's delusions, hallucinations, and daydreams—that it was good and even important to "abstain from the customary ways of making do." This was my first encounter with rhetoric and the persuasive powers of literary description. I probably couldn't say what it all amounted to, but I bought the book—the first book I remember buying of my own volition—and started reading it while standing outside my mother's hairdressing salon. It was late fall and cold, Rochester/ Canadian cold, and the light was fading, and my hands were trembling, but I read without realizing I was reading. I can't recall ever having done this before. My interest in the book was greater than the anxiety reading it caused.

This process of leaping over my own incapacities to the excitement in the narrator's voice is necessary every time I find my mind wandering away from something I'm reading; it's a way of reading intuitively, and emotionally. To this day the act of reading is never anything less than challenging.

This was also the first time I was aware of the presence of a first-person persona narrator, the very first time I was transported by the charm and existential detachment of someone's written voice. Binx Bolling, Percy's wise, self-referential gentlemanly narrator and main character, was speaking directly to me about his love for his second cousin, his profoundly dispirited soulmate, Kate. The particular quality of his conversational voice made me feel less alone, as if I'd found the friend I'd been looking for all my life. And Binx's honest, unadorned self-assessments seemed to be my own; his lack of confidence or willingness to commit to any particular ideal matched my own frazzled sense of self. I seemed to be "listening" (not reading) to a voice in my own head, to a personage invented by my own fantasies. I read the entire novel straight through in three days and two nights, and though I couldn't say exactly what it was about or what Mr. Percy meant me to understand, I was reading emotionally, using the power of my imagination, intuition, and sensibilities to understand and decode written language. And what language it was!

I was enjoying the "process" of reading beyond anything I'd previously believed possible.

7

WHEN I WAS TWENTY AND A COLLEGE STUDENT IN San Francisco a therapist told me that given my obvious intelligence I should be able to understand something easily enough. I can still feel the weight and taste of each word: *given my obvious intelligence.*

My intelligence?

At the time I was living in an attic room, caring part-time for an autistic boy in return for my room and board. I bussed dishes in the school cafeteria while serving as a teaching assistant to two of my writing teachers. My desire to overcome this image of myself as a member of the Dummy Class carried me though these times. I told myself one way or another I would be a writer, a good one, the same way I'd taught myself to read. With much to prove, I felt deliberate, stubborn, determined, and maybe even a little crazy—who else but the crazy expect so much from so little, ignore the odds of playing against a stacked deck in favor of—Billy's dictum—going headlong or not going at all? Yet never once did it occur to me that I was intelligent.

"Do you really think that—that I'm intelligent?" I asked her. She hadn't given me any tests—how did she know for sure? There seemed to be so much proof to the contrary.

Later, a graduate student at the University of Iowa, fearing I would fail a required linguistics class and not get my degree, I tried to get out of the class by seeking as an exemption the Old and Middle English classes I'd taken as an undergraduate. The professor, a kindly man nearing retirement age, possessed of a much admired ironic disposition (his class was mysteriously given at 8:30 a.m., providing him with the occasion to quip: "I go to bed late, but not *that* late!"), smiled as I made my pitch in his office. He'd obviously heard my arguments many times before. Interrupting my plea, he suddenly asked what a phoneme was. "If you don't need to take linguistics, surely you know what one is, Mr. Schultz."

I failed high school Latin twice, survived two years of college French with C-'s by memorizing the text and never going to class, a semester of German (quitting midterm), a number of Old and Middle English classes (which I passed only because I loved the wonderful poetry the gifted professor sang aloud in class and didn't mind memorizing it), and one semester of a logic class. I'd come into contact with phonemes and probably would've come up with an acceptable version of the right answer (which is what he expected: an acceptable answer that would allow him to grant me the exemption) if it weren't for the anxiety his question caused me. I assumed my not being able to answer meant that I was *not* intelligent, and that this was exactly what he was trying to demonstrate. I ran out of his office before he could offer me an exemption. He later explained in a note he was only attempting to let me know that linguistics was of some importance to a writer.

Later, I would learn that foreign languages are particularly difficult for dyslexics. Many specialists believe learning a foreign language for a dyslexic is a form of abuse. As far as I was concerned, linguistics was a foreign language, as demanding and stressful as the Latin class I failed twice. According to the International Dyslexia Association, foreign-language teachers aren't trained to identify or deal with learning needs, or to provide the necessary accommodations. Their use of language labs, listening tapes, oral communication, and computer-assisted learning only serve normal learners and are "detrimental to the at-risk learner" who needs a more "systematic, structured, multisensory approach."

I now understand that my intelligence wasn't the reason I couldn't keep up with the pace of the foreign-language courses I took, or why I couldn't respond when called upon, or repeat words that had "sounds or phonemes that have little or no resemblance to the native language," as the International Dyslexia Association explains. Listening to someone speak French on a language tape was a torture to me. This is why I couldn't *hear* a single word or identify phrases, and why I could never under any circumstances understand or apply grammatical rules or recognize spelling patterns. I actually did know what a phoneme was—a fundamental element of all spoken and written words, fashioned out of the forty-four basic phoneme combos from which Shakespeare, Dante, and Emily Dickinson worked their magic. What I didn't know was where my dyslexia stopped and some bizarre emotional problem began. If I kept running out of rooms every time someone asked me something I couldn't process, I not only wouldn't get a degree, I wouldn't get or hold a job, or any semblance of self-respect.

One in every five children suffers from some form of dyslexia, while millions of others struggle to read at their grade level. Dr. Sally Shaywitz, a neuroscientist and professor of pediatrics at Yale, and the author of the extremely useful and comprehensive book *Overcoming Dyslexia,* explains that we arrive in the world knowing how to speak, but reading is an acquired act, "an invention that must be learned at a conscious level." It is the naturalness of speaking that makes reading so hard, a reader must "convert the print on a page into a linguistic code—the phonetic code," and if he can't, these letters remain a blur devoid of any recognizable pattern, or meaning. The linguist Leonard Bloomfeld put it this way: "Writing is not language, but merely a way of recording language by visible marks." We've had a written language for five thousand years, while speech has evolved over the last fifty thousand years. Writing language demands work, practice, and determination even for the learners.

In addressing the difficulty dyslexics encounter in learning a foreign language, Dr. Shaywitz tells us, "persistent difficulties . . . provide an important clue that a student may be dyslexic," and "a person who has not mastered the phonetic code and developed into a skilled reader must rely on brute memorization." Brute memorization is how

I passed Latin and French, and managed to finally pass the courses while quickly forgetting what I learned. "There is one final clue to dyslexia in children and adults alike: the fact that they say they are in pain. Dyslexia inflicts pain. It represents a major assault on self-esteem. In grade school children, this may be expressed as a reluctance to attend school or moodiness or spoken expressions such as 'I'm dumb' or 'I get teased a lot,'" Dr. Shaywitz tells us, whereas "adolescents may develop feelings of shame and work hard to hide their reading problem by avoiding school, pretending to have forgotten assignments, and doing anything not to read aloud in class. Adults invariably harbor deep pain and sadness reflecting years of assaults to their sense of self-worth."

I was moved to tears when I first read this. I already knew it firsthand, but reading it—being *able* to read it—allowed me to see my dyslexia from a new and scientific perspective, and this made all the difference in the world. Pain is always there, near the surface, ready to assert itself in demeaning, shameful memories, but I know now that this isn't a matter of low intelligence, as it isn't for all the other children and adolescents who struggle to decode language. It's a matter of neurology, science, and pain. One's self-image is a very fragile and private thing. On the most intimate level of all, the level of self-worth, every dyslexic owns a history of self-rejection and regret. It can be addressed and understood over time, but it cannot be erased. My image of myself as a dummy is neurologically, phonologically, linguistically wired into the core of my being. It is my phonetic code. When I read, this image of myself reads along with me, interpreting each word, each phoneme. If my ambition as a writer is to overcome this image, it is a futile one.

8

ONE OF MY FATHER'S NIECES WAS A SUBSTITUTE
teacher at my school so it wasn't surprising that everyone
in the family seemed to know about my learning problems. I discovered this when we went to Passover dinner
at my father's sister's house during my first year at my
new school. Being the youngest at the table, I was asked
to read from the Haggadah in Hebrew. This too was
surprising because everyone there knew I couldn't read
Hebrew and I'd always read my part in English, which
made me anxious enough. When I refused, my cousin—
older than me by four years, and someone who practiced
the art of bullying with great skill and pleasure—asked
if it was because I was in the Dummy Class and couldn't
read English? Usually he insulted me in private. Unable
to respond, I looked down at my hands. "But your father

tells everyone how smart you are—what is a genius doing with dummies?"

My father told a lot of lies: everyone at his vending locations believed we lived in the suburbs and that I went to a private school. The difference between the world he imagined for us and the one we lived in, was a running joke among his brothers and sisters, all of whom somehow managed to live in nice houses in the suburbs. And now I was being shown to be one of his lies. Everyone looked as if they were waiting for me to say something in my defense. But what could I say—it was true, I couldn't learn Hebrew for the same reason I couldn't learn English, or anything else. And not knowing Hebrew felt even worse. It was a failure not only in my eyes and the eyes of my parents but in the eyes of God too. Perhaps this was why my parents sat there looking at their hands, saying nothing on my behalf. The bullying and mockery was deserved. It was my obligation as a Jew, and a member of a tribe as old as civilization itself, to understand the language of the Bible. But I could think of nothing to say so once again I got up and ran away, this time outside into a blizzard without even thinking to look for my coat. The snow came to my knees. I slogged down the middle of the unplowed street and tried to imagine what it would feel like to read Hebrew—I knew some of the Passover songs by heart, having memorized them in transliteration, but not being able to read them excluded me in the most personal manner. I felt enslaved to my ignorance. It was only fitting that this was Passover, a time to memorialize a people's pursuit of freedom from bondage, and ignorance was certainly a form of bondage. I couldn't bear being perceived as too stupid to be a Jew. I walked until I couldn't feel my hands and feet, and when my father's car pulled up alongside me I climbed in, and sat in the backseat. I stared out the window into the vast unrelenting whiteness of a world whose mysteries were all written in a language I couldn't understand.

I love Judaism's great traditions and rituals, its ancient original way of thinking and apprehending culture, its affirming unparalleled belief in praise and celebration, which against all odds has prevailed for millennia. I appreciate the significance of its sustaining laws and precepts. Being a Jew is no small part of my identity, as a man and a writer, but I never feel more apart and isolated than when I am among my fellow Jews in a place of worship, when the congregation is reading and speaking Hebrew. It's impossible for me to be there without feeling inferior and bewildered.

Sheldon Zimmerman, the rabbi at my temple, where my oldest son had his bar mitzvah and my youngest son is studying toward his, recently told me how deeply spiritual he found my writing. Although I write about being Jewish in a cultural and historical context—in *Living in the Past* I wrote a book-length autobiographical poetry sequence about the year in a boy's life leading up to his bar mitzvah—I'm not religious in any formal sense and don't see myself as consciously writing from a "spiritual" or even particularly Jewish perspective. When I wrote fiction I was deeply influenced and affected by Jewish writers like Bellow, Malamud, Babel, and Roth, but I've never seen myself as a "Jewish" writer.

Rabbi Zimmerman smiled when I said something to this effect. He knows that, except for the years leading up to Eli's bar mitzvah, I go to temple only on the High Holidays; that I go to hear the wonderful language and music of the prayers, and listen to our gifted cantor sing. What he doesn't know—because I've never told anyone other than my wife—is that I go despite the fact that my initial reaction to stepping into a room filled with strangers is absolute dread. Add the significant conundrum of it being a Jewish ceremony and my anxiety is sometimes unbearable. I feel I must pretend to be knowledgeable about something I know almost nothing about. I've made many attempts over the years to learn about Judaism and probably know more about it than I can admit to myself, but none of this makes any difference. The more I learn about my religion, the more ignorant and unworthy I feel. It's a paradox I've suffered all my life. When I go to temple I do so because it feels worse not to go. While in college and graduate school, I attended Passover services a few times—often out of loneliness and homesickness—but it wasn't until I married that I began to regularly attend services at my temple. My wife and I joined so that our children could be bar mitzvahed; they could then decide for themselves how religious they would be. Being a Jew for your children is less complicated, and in my case less conflicted, than being one for myself.

Now I know that the real reason I never felt I belonged to this world of the faithful and the devout is that I must stand there among so many others not knowing what they know, and hating myself with an ardor that feels as old as the language itself, isolated by my ignorance.

Judaism is a world constituted almost entirely of language: the ancient beautiful language of the Jews. Our synagogue is reformed and therefore more relaxed in its adherence to the laws and principles of Judaism, but it makes little difference. It's a world of passion for its own history of laws and faith and learning—all recorded in a language invented out of this very passion. It's a language derived directly out of the heart of the mind and translated and coded in music indigenous only to itself—the infinitely mysterious and beautiful music of a people who strove to understand their suffering in order to give it meaning.

One Yom Kippur, in a great tent holding nearly two thousand people during the High Holidays, I stood at the end of a row of people holding a prayer book, pretending to be reading and singing along like someone who never for a moment doubted where he belonged. I was both a man in my fifties standing in a tent filled with other worldly men and women from Manhattan, and also a boy of ten sitting in a balcony under the chipped peeling ceiling of the Big Shul with my grandma and all the other old immigrant women who spoke not a sentence of English nor knew one word of their ancient language but attended despite their segregation and ignorance, because it was the one place in the history of the world they knew where they felt accepted and at home. My father and mother never set foot in a synagogue. I was too young to sit by myself downstairs with the men, pious and important in a

82

faith I feared I would never myself own. On Yom Kippur, the evening of Nol Kidre when the music and enthrallment of the idea of atonement and humility under God is most intense and therefore most splendid, surrounded by men and women moving to a music only they could hear, their eyes shut and faces lifted up toward the ceiling, I so desperately wished I could read the prayers I could almost taste the Hebrew words on my tongue.

Later that night, I wrote this poem, which perhaps caused Rabbi Zimmerman to say what he did to me:

YOM KIPPUR

You are asked to stand and bow your head,
consider the harm you've caused,
the respect you've withheld,
the anger misspent, the fear spread,
the earnestness displayed
in the service of prestige and sensibility,
all the callous, cruel, stubborn, joyless sins
in your alphabet of woe
so that you might be forgiven.
You are asked to believe in the spark
of your divinity, in the purity

of the words of your mouth
and the memories of your heart.
You are asked for this one day and one night
to starve your body so your soul can feast
on faith and adoration.
You are asked to forgive the past
and remember the dead, to gaze
across the desert in your heart
toward Jerusalem. To separate
the sacred from the profane
and be as numerous as the sands
and the stars of heaven.
To believe that no matter what
you have done to yourself and others
morning will come and the mountain
of night will fade. To believe,
for these few precious moments,
in the utter sweetness of your life.
You are asked to bow your head
and remain standing,
and say Amen.

The speaker in the poem is someone who understands
the meaning and mystery of this day, and never doubts

that he belongs there. He is part of the place and the idea of the ceremony. He knows the utter sweetness of his life. I was so taken with the beautiful music of the ceremony I created a persona narrator who felt entitled to express what I was feeling underneath all my misgivings. I created someone who wasn't an outsider, who felt privileged to be there. People have written me to say the poem is read on Yom Kippur in their synagogues. Rabbi Zimmerman asked me to read it to our congregation on Yom Kippur this year. Later that night an Israeli friend wrote to say his rabbi read the poem to his Conservative congregation in Jerusalem. Because only one third of the three hundred people in his Conservative Synagogue were English-speaking, the poem had been translated into Hebrew, and his rabbi wanted to know if I'd originally written it in Hebrew, it sounded to his rabbi as if it had been. There's great irony here, of course, but also great satisfaction, and pleasure. My persona had convinced an Israeli rabbi not only that he was entitled to these feelings of faith, but also that he could speak Hebrew, that he could sing from his heart of the sorrow and foreboding and fretful jubilation of this most holy of days, and in Jerusalem of all places.

9

YEHUDA AMICHAI, THE GREAT ISRAELI POET, ONCE told me that my soul was older and more Jewish than his, but that he never met someone who knew less about the Bible and being a Jew. We would laugh at the idea of someone like this being burdened with such a soul. Was this a trick of God, to give an ancient, pure soul to someone who couldn't appreciate it? It was an idea out of Isaac Bashevis Singer or Sholem Aleichem.

Yehuda lived among Jews all his life. He was born in Germany but lived in Israel since the age of thirteen, before it was a nation. The fact that he claimed he hadn't met my kind before was somehow both pleasing and disconcerting. He didn't understand why I hadn't bothered to study my people as he had. And I couldn't explain because then I didn't understand it myself.

He tried more than once to teach me a few words in Hebrew. He was a patient and kind teacher, pronouncing each syllable slowly and fully, with all the rich intonations of his wonderful speaking voice. But it never did any good. I couldn't re-create his sounds, or even remember the words he was trying to teach me. I don't know how much I was affected by my memories of my failures in Hebrew school, but every time I tried to replicate the sound of a word he pronounced my mind shut down, and I heard only its echo. He wanted me to know something of my ancient language, hoping that once I did I would fall in love with its music and learn it the way one learns to love a woman. I was lucky to have such a guide—and later I did go on to learn much more about Judaism and the Bible with his prompting—but to this day I regret that I wasn't able to explain that my ignorance about learning Hebrew wasn't a matter of choice. There were times when my frustration reached a point where I would pretend to be speaking Hebrew, making hard guttural noises and trying to look like someone who was actually speaking Hebrew. This would get a big laugh from him, his wife Hana, and their children, Ron, David, and Emanuella, but it wasn't a joking matter to me; it was an attempt to mask my disappointment, and frustration, and shame.

Here is a section of Yehuda's great book-length poem sequence *Open Closed Open,* his last book translated and published in the United States:

7 (OF "ISRAELI TRAVEL: OTHERNESS IS ALL, OTHERNESS IS LOVE")

I passed by the school where I studied as a boy
and said in my heart: Here I learned certain things
and not others. All my life I have loved in vain
the things I didn't learn. I am filled with knowledge,
good and evil, I know all about its flowering,
the shape of its leaves, the function of its root system, its
     pests and parasites.
I am still studying good and evil, and will go on studying
     till the day I die.
I stood near the school building. This is the room
where we sat and studied. Classroom windows always open
to the future, but in our innocence we thought it was
     landscape
we were seeing through the window.
The schoolyard was narrow, paved with large stones.
I remember the brief tumult of the two of us
near the rickety steps, the tumult

that was the beginning of a first great love.
Now it outlives us, as if in a museum,
like everything else in Jerusalem.

"All my life I have loved in vain / the things I didn't learn." If only I could've accomplished this victory of bliss over ignorance. Yehuda was a great artist of profound feeling expressed directly, but he was also an artist of implication and metaphor—he's speaking in the poem not only of those specific things he didn't learn but of the larger mysteries of life which we cannot bring ourselves to know: good and evil, what the future holds, the burden of loss, death, and the special secret knowledge that love brings. In the English translation the music is soulful and ever-building, but I cannot bring myself to even imagine what it must sound like in its original modern Hebrew—this is a regret I must live with like a wound.

ONCE, WHILE STAYING WITH HIM IN JERUSALEM, WE visited the Holocaust Memorial at Yad Vashem. At one of the exhibits, while listening to recordings in various languages reciting the details of children killed in German death camps, I wanted so passionately to understand a recording in Hebrew about a particular Polish child killed in Auschwitz that I became overwhelmed and ran outside into the blistering sunlight. Surely it was partly the grief of being in a place that so thoroughly recorded the history of atrocity perpetrated on Jews that made me flee, but my flight also came as a direct result of my frustration in not understanding the precise details about this Polish child. Yehuda found me and stood with me on a balcony, overlooking the beautiful hills of Jerusalem. His arm around me, we stood in a silence filled with awe and grief.

"Philip, are you okay?" he asked.

Unable to speak, I nodded. The intensity of my response had alarmed him. I don't remember what I was feeling but no doubt it involved a belief that this grief could be understood only in its true and original language and that my ignorance was another kind of exile. I wish I knew then what I do now about how my dyslexia affected my not being able to learn Hebrew. It would've made a great difference if I could've explained this to Yehuda, but I think he understood. Grief was an essential part of our friendship, a bond we shared the way we shared our sense of irony and desire to celebrate even those things we loved but couldn't learn. I finally asked him what was said about the child killed in Auschwitz and when he told me we both wept. Standing beside him, who sang so powerfully of this place, its beauty and timelessness, I felt, for this one moment at least, that my soul also was ancient and Jewish and at home.

I O

FOR MUCH OF MY LIFE I UNDERSTOOD MYSELF PRI-
marily in psychological terms. My problems in school
were a consequence of the disappointments of my immigrant family; I was a product, and to some extent a
victim, of my peasant world and low self-esteem. My
self-awareness was fashioned by years of psychotherapy
and the self-analysis and introspection necessary to the
writing of poetry. Now I understand that my dyslexia
has played an equally important role in my development,
both as a poet and a teacher of writing. It feels as if I'm
meeting myself for the first time.

When I first started teaching college in the mid-
seventies I noticed that nearly all of my poetry and fiction students were using the same autobiographical "I"
(or "me") they used to write their diaries, journals, and

letters. These narrators were stand-ins for themselves and allowed them little or no distance from their characters. Once they understood that writers like Salinger, Philip Roth, and Chekhov used invented narrators—with attitudes and dilemmas different from their own—there was a remarkable improvement in their work. Holden Caulfield, Huck Finn, and Hemingway's Jake Barnes gave their authors a remove in which they could "see" their characters as actors in their stories. It isn't as obvious in poems, but the same principle pertains: the poetic "I" isn't really the poet, it's a made-up persona or personality possessing a perspective, distance, and sympathy for its characters that often changes from poem to poem.

In the famous Robert Frost poem "Stopping by Woods on a Snowy Evening," the speaker begins: "Whose woods these are I think I know." Clearly Frost isn't using his own speaking voice, but a persona of great focus and intimacy to set up a scene and tell a story through his masterful use of rhyme and meter. When the speaker tells us that "My little horse must think it queer / To stop without a farmhouse near," he isn't only describing the place, he's revealing the personality of his "I" so that the reader will identify with him and believe in the urgency of a carefully constructed narrator who tells us:

The woods are lovely, dark, and deep,
But I have promises to keep,
And miles to go before I sleep,
And miles to go before I sleep.

The music and wonderful simplicity work their magic, of course, but it's the persuasive sincerity and authority of his narrator that is most memorable.

When I discovered that my most persuasive narrators were the ones whose personal agendas and attitudes were most different from my own, I started "borrowing" narrators from my favorite writers. The famous opening of Saul Bellow's novel *The Adventures of Augie March* is a good example. "I am an American, Chicago born—Chicago, that somber city—and go at things as I have taught myself, free-style, and will make the record in my own way: first to knock, first admitted. . . ." I always imagined this was Bellow's own voice until I noticed how similar it is to Ishmael's in Melville's *Moby-Dick*, which begins: "Call me Ishmael. Some years ago—never mind how long precisely—having little or no money in my purse, and nothing particular to interest me on shore, I thought I would sail about a little and see the watery part of the world . . . it is a damp, drizzly November in my soul. . . ." These forthright and high-minded narrators, written nearly a century apart, equipped with outsize personalities of great brio and intellectual capacity, are not only perfectly suited to their stories, they're undeniably similar. Yes, Bellow knew his Melville as Melville knew his Bible.

Inspired, I borrowed one of Chekhov's curiously self-obsessed busybody narrators for a poem about my experience working as a clerk in a welfare building in San Francisco in the sixties. I'd tried using this material in novels, play, stories, and poems but I could never bring the building's atmosphere of relentless despair to life. The narrators I was using were all the same clueless "I" (or "me") who was being driven crazy dodging the Vietnam War and trying to survive a world of constant sexual and spiritual upheaval. A therapist I was seeing quipped: "How can you write a novel while you're so busy living one?" Chekhov's narrators were good at revealing their narrator's inner life without telling us more than we needed to know. The young nobleman in "Agafya" was perfect: "During my stay in the S— district, I often used to visit Savva Stukach, or simply Savka, at the Dubrovsk allotments. These allotments were my favorite spot for so-called 'general' fishing, when, on leaving home, you don't know on what day or at what hour you will be back, and you take all the fishing tackle you can lay your hands on, as well as enough food to last you for days." What previously comprised hundreds of pages about my various agonized states of mind was now a poem of five quatrains:

BALANCE

Eight years gone & the welfare building is a parking ramp.
The attendant can't recall where it went. Uptown some-
    where, he thinks.
But ten thousand people filled these halls & only the ocean
is a carpet big enough to sweep so many under.

I was a clerk who read Chekhov & knew the fate of clerks.
I learned to sway down halls like a dancer & never stop to
    listen.
Mornings I filed dental reports & wore earplugs against
    the crying
for crutches, steel hands & mattresses fitted to broken backs.

A Mrs. Montvale perched on my desk & swore she'd kill
    herself
if her new dentures didn't arrive by Thanksgiving.

A fatalist with rotting gums, she feared dying toothless at
   a feast.
Near closing time the ghosts lined up around the block,
   still waiting.

In Central Index I watched the hundred Ferris wheels
flip rainbow cards sorting the dead from the quickly dying
& filed the electric buzz of computers into a symphony so
   grand
it washed the curdled voices from my head.

I'm glad the building's gone. Despair can't be tolerated
in such numbers & Gray's *Anatomy* doesn't explain
how the human body breaks a hundred ways each day &
   still finds balance.
Lord of Mercy, the dead still need bus fare & salvation!

This technique is basically the same one I used to
teach myself how to read. I would lie in bed trying to
imagine what it would feel like to be able to read, to be
normal enough to be like every other child in the world.
I would lie there with my mother staring at the words in
the comic books pretending I was reading them myself.

I didn't know it at the time but I was inventing a boy who didn't suffer from dyslexia, who was "normal." I was creating a narrator capable of rewriting my story with a happy ending.

To this day, when I'm too tired to teach or play with my sons after a long day of work, I do the same thing—I find an energetic persona prescient, intuitive, and durable enough to do what I fear I can't. The method of teaching I've created at the Writers Studio, my school, built on this philosophy, is another example of my thinking in a compensatory roundabout byzantine manner, the way of the dyslexic mind.

I I

I RECENTLY ASKED MY WIFE WHAT IT WAS LIKE LIVING
with two dyslexics. I wasn't being facetious or ironic, it
just suddenly occurred to me to wonder. I already knew
something about having a dyslexic son, but what was
it like having to live with two people struggling with
all the difficulties of a learning disability? The look on
her face said everything. The kind of daily support she
has provided our son and myself has without a doubt
been challenging. I know that her availability to discuss
the revelations I've come to in writing about dyslexia
has made a difficult process possible. At the very least,
the processing problems and endless research of necessary information (such as getting the right teachers and
tutors), planning playdates and sleepovers with appropriate

friends, establishing workable house rules to avoid conflicts, while making sure our youngest boy, Augie, who doesn't have a learning disability, isn't being left out of the mix—all demand her constant attention.

Last summer, for instance, while we were hiking in the Shenandoah National Park, Augie, overhearing an argument between me and his brother about which path to take back to the trailhead, shook his head with a world-weariness unusual for a ten-year-old, and said, "It's all about the dyslexics."

His comment was both hilarious and moving—how many dinners has he had to sit through enduring the complications and challenges his brother and I face, while his mother tried to mediate and offer help? It certainly helps matters that he's talented athletically and does well in school. But here we were, on vacation in the Blue Ridge Mountains, one of the most beautiful places in America, and he had to listen to a heated argument about whether the map said to turn right or left. His comment was not only pithy and perceptive; it summed up what has to be the constant patience, sympathy, and understanding that living with dyslexics requires.

The toll on families with learning disabled children is well documented. Many high schools require a foreign language, which places an extra burden on the amount of homework the students have to do, and an additional expense for educational tutoring. Psychological support is also needed to address the bullying and self-esteem issues so many dyslexic children must endure. For the most part, I had to manage on my own, but this is not always possible today. Many kids with dyslexia manage to compensate for their limitations and diminish their own pain by seeking sympathy, or displaying empathy for the pain of others.

This kind of sympathy is not easily summoned. Sometimes I saw myself through the eyes of those who taunted me. There were other times when I felt more sympathy for my tormentors than I did for myself. It's been a great help to think that I might have something of value to say to the many others who struggle with learning disabilities, others who may not have been as fortunate in understanding and overcoming them.

When I taught poetry writing in grade schools I used the children's enthusiasm as a resource. Though many of their other teachers later came to enjoy the "magic" their students performed in class—perhaps, because of the "creative" focus of my job—they were often suspicious of me. What could this poet from New York City do that they couldn't? What was the purpose of teaching something as arcane and elitist as poetry in often overcrowded classes when so many of their students struggled with the basics? Although I didn't know about my dyslexia then, I did know that I would've loved being taught how to write creatively. I would've loved to learn to put words together with feelings, through poetry.

Appealing to a child's imagination is perhaps the best way of fostering confidence in children. Kids who have already learned to mistrust their learning abilities can be reached through their love of surprise. I was often moved by the reaction of these children to my faith in their ability to climb the ladder of their own imaginative thinking. I didn't know that in teaching poetry I was reaching back toward the frightened lost child I'd been in order to rescue him.

Most teachers of writing teach what they learned though long trial and error, many prefer to work with those students who best reflect their own accomplishments. I work with gifted students, but I also work with those students who don't always readily shine. I work especially hard with those who—like me—have to fight tooth and nail to make any progress at all. In some ways, my method of teaching is designed with these students in mind. A number of years ago the head of a prestigious writing program told me he believed the job of writing programs was to sort out the gifted from the merely serviceable. Surprised, I thought of *my place* in grade school. I asked him if he felt any responsibility to those others who don't demonstrate quickly an apparent gift, and if he ever feared he was failing them. His smile was answer enough. He didn't, not for a moment.

Albert Einstein, also dyslexic, said he wasn't the smartest person he knew—others had higher IQs—but he was the most creative. It's hard not to wonder what role his dyslexia played in his very original way of thinking. Dyslexics have to make up a great deal from scratch as they go along. Our minds turn most things into a game of one-upmanship in which blame is the main currency. Knowing this has been useful to me in teaching others to find their own formulas for emotional connection. Knowing something about the role fear played in my life, and the extent to which I was controlled by it, has given me insight into the length others go to avoid their own vulnerable feelings. I believe fear is the main reason why the majority of students stop writing, and why others are reluctant to write about those subjects they feel most passionately about. The Writers Studio is approaching its twenty-fourth year and not one of those years has gone by without some serious reassessment of its approach. I think of a line by Baudelaire: "The dispersion and reconstitution of the self. That's the whole story." We are constantly making and remaking and unmaking ourselves, an endless process of dispersion in which we find and lose ourselves in the current of an ever-changing story. A reconstitution of the self, and finding the right narrator to tell its story, is what I am attempting to do as a writer and a teacher. I no longer find it surprising that someone should feel little sympathy for a character with whom he most identifies. It's only surprising when he does.

My way of teaching is a long, intriguing, and complicated system of support. It sometimes seems as if I'm in the business of convincing people that they in fact possess the strength to reveal, in their work, the mystery of their nature. Great art does precisely that. Dyslexics perform some version of this in order to survive. Art's power of persuasion resides in the small personal details of one's own story, and if it weren't for my struggle with dyslexia, I doubt I'd ever have become a writer or known how to teach others to write.

IN A SENSE, DYSLEXICS ARE CONDITIONED BY THEIR environments to blame only themselves for their learning difficulties. Interview any dyslexic and you'll soon discover a world of blame, guilt, and shame. This is certainly different for children who know early on that they're dyslexic and get help and support, though perhaps not entirely. For a child to know they're different and be branded as such from other children is always painful. Richard Lavoie, who has worked as a teacher and headmaster at residential special education facilities for the last thirty years, tells us in his very insightful book *It's So Much Work to Be Your Friend* that "once a child develops a reputation among his peers—particularly a *negative* reputation—it becomes his indelible label. Unlike most adults, children are relatively inflexible and unforgiving in regard to interpersonal relationships. Once they brand a peer a 'loser' or a 'nerd,' they tend to interpret and evaluate all of their interactions with that child through that 'filter.' The child's positive behaviors are ignored, while his mistakes and miscues are viewed as evidence that the loser label is accurate and fitting."

To some extent, this must be true also of a child's interpretations and evaluations of his own behavior. It was certainly true in my case. Once branded a dummy, always a dummy.

Not very long ago I got stuck trying to pronounce the word "arthritic" while reading my poem "The Magic Kingdom." I was reading with poets I admired and as soon as I couldn't identify the word I forgot how to pronounce it, and panicked. The line reads: *these arthritic animals tag behind:*

> *I never thought I'd have so much to give up;*
> *that the view from this side of my life*
> *would be so precious. Bless*
> *these filaments of sea glass,*
> *this chorus of piping plovers*
> *and bickering wrens, each mile*
> *these arthritic animals tag behind,*
> *sniffing tire ruts, frothy craters of rotting driftwood,*
> *lacy seaweed and scuttling crabs,*
> *after someone deliciously foul. . . .*

While writing, I usually select words based on how their sound affects the sound of every other word in the line. Occasionally, although I try not to, I'll select a word because it's easy to pronounce. I was wary of using the word "arthritic" because I sometimes put an extra syllable in *arthritis,* pronouncing it *arthuritis,* as if it contained the name Arthur. I often add or subtract syllables in words without knowing I'm doing it. When reading the poem at a poetry reading I'm usually aware that I'm approaching the word and prepare myself, but this time I lost track of it until I heard myself mispronouncing it, first in my imagination, and then in the actual line. To make matters worse, instead of simply skipping over it and moving on, I stood in a daze, staring down at a blizzard of unintelligible black marks on the page, mispronouncing it over and over again. Afterwards, the organizer of the event asked me if anything like this had ever happened before. I lied and said no, probably because I was too shaken to tell the truth. It wasn't until well into my ride back home to East Hampton that I wondered if my not being able to pronounce the word had anything to do with my dyslexia.

I refused to read my work in public all through college out of fear of stuttering; stage fright, I told myself, a bad case of the willies. But readings are an important part of a professional poet's life, and when I had to promote my first book, I would get slightly drunk before each reading, hoping it might take the edge off my nervousness. Alcohol and dyslexia is a lethal combination that only exacerbates the processing problems; the illusion of calm alcohol temporarily provides is only that, an illusion. I can't even have a glass of wine before a reading; afterwards I'll reward myself with a glass, but never before.

Knowing about my dyslexia, I'm somewhat more forgiving now. I smile to think of other mishaps during readings—the time I lost my place in a poem and ended up reading the end of a different poem without knowing it. The result was so "surreal" people later came up to say how much they liked my new style. Or when my stuttering triggered a bad case of the hiccups, the combination causing such merriment, even I couldn't help laughing at the idea of someone struggling not to succumb to one ailment, while being possessed by another. Later, while attempting to console me, a friend reminded me that the German poet Rilke would get nosebleeds during readings. What were hiccups compared to that! It wasn't very comforting.

If I'm asked to introduce another writer at a reading, I type and print out my introductions, because speaking extemporaneously often triggers a medley of confused tenses and names, a labyrinth of self-corrections and regretful thoughts. While teaching, I sometimes forget what I'm attempting to say and sometimes mangle metaphors and clichés. Identifying the cliché—and they do have their usefulness in teaching because of their love of the common denominator—I'm after has become something of a game to my good-natured, patient students: you can lead a horse where and then do what with it—it's better to be what than whom? When I sit down to write, a tentative bartering goes on in my mind, a trade-off between agitation and a compensatory rerouting of intentions, which more often than not leaves me exhausted and occasionally elated. The urge to get up, water my plants, heat my tea is often too powerful to resist. And when I can trick my mind into making something out of nothing, into putting words to thought, and accented thought to music, there soon follows in time a walloping sense of forlornness and dread. Perhaps this forlornness is the price every artist must pay for the privilege and pleasures of being creative? It certainly isn't an uncommon experience for writers, or limited to those suffering from dyslexia. But for dyslexics it goes with the territory. In fact, it is the territory.

12

IN THE SEVENTIES, WHEN I WAS LIVING IN CAMBRIDGE, Massachusetts, my agent at the time phoned to say the editor he sent my novel to liked it very much. It was a late Friday afternoon and my agent said he'd known the editor a long time and that it was 97 percent final they would publish it and I should go out and celebrate. I called friends who offered to throw a party for me. The editor wouldn't have expressed such excitement without being certain, one said. This kind of endorsement meant they would get behind the book. My girlfriend stood in the doorway, smiling at me. It was early spring and I sat looking out the window at the fading light, feeling I had everything I wanted. I next called my mother, who was still living in Rochester, in a city-operated retirement complex. In a few more years she would come down with

Alzheimer's, but her mind was perfectly clear that afternoon. "See," she laughed, "and they said you couldn't be a writer. Boy, did you show them!" Remembering Mr. Joyce, we both laughed.

"Philip," my mother said, "did I ever tell you what the psychologist told me when you got held back?"

"No," I said, not sure I wanted to know.

"She said they'd taken tests and you were more than smart enough to read. She made it sound like it was your fault. That you didn't want to learn to read."

"I must've thought the same thing," I said.

"Boy, did you show her!"

It was a party to remember. Everyone was happy for me.

On Monday my agent called to say the editor had changed his mind, he still thought highly of the novel, but his colleagues didn't think it was publishable in its present form. I thought of my conversation with my mother and wondered if that school shrink wasn't right after all: maybe I *was* responsible for the endless variety of my predicaments.

I'm now sitting in my study in East Hampton, several hundred miles and some thirty-six years distant from that particular moment in Cambridge, and I finally understand that the life of an artist is in many ways similar to the life of the dyslexic. Both are essentially dysfunctional systems that produce in each individual volumes of anxiety, perseverance, and rejection, as well as creative compensatory thinking. Each, by their very nature, makes a victim of its creator, turning him into an outsider and misfit. It's true of all artists, I think, at every level of success, the more gifted, the greater and riskier the anxiety and struggle. Each must, without appeal, strive to tolerate its own forms of self-defamation, creative excitement, and lack of forgiveness.

My poetry, like my dyslexia, serves as a giant filter for my darkest feelings and ideas. Sooner or later everything of consequence passes through this filter. Everyone who suffers mild, or seriously debilitating, non-verbal or language-learning disabilities has trouble comprehending "the big picture." Doubt is its silent partner, its secret sharer. There's no little irony in the fact that the very things I couldn't do have helped provide me with a profession and means of knowing myself; that I chose to master the very thing that once hindered and mastered me; to own what once owned me.

PEOPLE OFTEN ASK ME WHEN AND HOW I KNEW I WAS a poet. There are several fancy responses and explanations but one certainly has to do with my longing for solitude. I can spend inordinate amounts of time alone in a room, living entirely in my thoughts and feelings.

I staved off boredom as a child by telling my grandma stories as my mother listened from the dining room, where she counted coins from my father's vending machines. We'd sit on the tiny blue sofa in the living room, which she used as a bed, and my grandma would listen intently, smiling and nodding, as my dreamy stories took us far away from our unhappy house in Rochester's inner city.

I can still see them in their peasant dresses surrounded by the drabness of the furniture and peeling wallpaper, and myself in their eyes, where to them I was more than what my performance in school described, more than what my teachers believed I was capable of, more than what I knew and didn't know about the real world. They knew who I was from my stories. And from the love they felt for me. There are times, while giving a reading, when I will catch myself looking for their faces in the audience. I'm looking for the comfort and encouragement memory provides, and the nostalgia of reclamation. We *are* the stories we tell, the things we make up and invent, we are more than the answers we give to questions, more even than our limitations—we are the cantankerous, infinitely mysterious dreams we somehow find the courage to imagine and sometimes to tell others.

Last March I attended a conference organized by Smart Kids with Learning Disabilities—a wonderful organization founded ten years ago by Jane Ross to support parents of children with dyslexia and attention deficit disorder—to accept an award. It was Smart Kids' tenth anniversary benefit, "The Sky's the Limit," at the Westport Country Playhouse, and we were there to celebrate our "talents in the arts, science, athletics and engineering." At the conference, I read the first chapter of this book and during a poetry book signing afterwards, inspired by what was seen as my having revealed a personal story, several parents of learning disabled children wanted to share with me their own stories. Bullying, one woman confided, made her move her daughter to four different schools in one year. A distinguished-looking man, a prominent lawyer, broke down while telling me what he had suffered seeing his son bullied and made fun of by his schoolmates. He'd been a high school football star and had made fun of other kids and felt he was paying the price for it now. It killed him to see his son suffer and nothing he did seemed to help. A woman of obvious intelligence and sophistication held my hand tightly as she described, with tears in her eyes, how her daughter refused to leave their house each morning to go to school. She said she cried and fought and locked herself in her room because kids tortured her about the way she spoke and looked and even walked. She pleaded with her parents to be home-schooled. One after another, these men and women felt compelled to tell me their stories. But I wasn't a stranger to these people. I was a fellow traveler down the same dark road, someone who understood. My wife and I looked at each other knowingly throughout each confession.

Of the many gifted children receiving awards that night, one in particular has made a lasting impression. Melissa Rey, sixteen, a high school sophomore in Manchester, Missouri, winner of the Youth Achievement Award, was diagnosed with dyslexia when she was in the first grade. Named "America's Top Young Scientist" in the 2008 Discover 3M Young Scientist Challenge at the NASA Space Center, she referred in her talk to her dyslexia as her secret weapon. She was making a distinction between herself and her non-learning disabled competitors. She said she had spent a good part of her life learning how to solve difficult problems, teaching herself how to think her way around obstacles, and she had recognized that her fellow applicants hadn't. They were doing what they always did, applying their high intelligence to a science and math problem, while she was using what had become a forceful solution to endless frustration to her advantage. She had earned this edge, this creative way of imagining her way through a dark wood, and now it was her secret source of confidence and inspiration. There weren't many dry eyes in the audience. We all understood what she was telling us. That even after everyone else seems to have given up on us, there remains some small part of us that continues to appreciate our capacity for renewal, and invention, and continues to feed our appetite for celebration. We alone know the delight of what we are capable of. I believe this with all my heart. Perhaps it is necessary to suffer greatly before we can reach this place of recognition and sensitivity, and appreciate what is special and worthwhile about us and behave accordingly.

Writers are archaeologists of their own souls. We dig until we hit bottom only to find there is another bottom underneath and another after that. We are capable of great harm and great sacrifice, but the point of this struggle must have something to do with not giving up. For a long time I couldn't imagine my life amounting to anything anyone else would view with respect and affection. I didn't know there was something wrong or different about how my brain processed information and language; I believed there was something wrong with *me*. I still, on occasion, believe this. Perhaps I always will. But even when the entire world seemed to be ganging up on me, some persisting sense of myself argued on my behalf. I can't say why exactly, though I've always believed what St. Augustine said to be true: "Everything that is, in so far as it is, is good." And what is good is worthwhile and prevailing. No matter how rich or powerful or intelligent or wise we are, we are also small and inconsequential and of no worth at all. Everyone knows this. But we endure. My son is special not despite, but because of, his dyslexia. He is learning he is good and capable the way an archaeologist learns the history of the earth, inch by deliberate and all-consuming inch; the way we all learn to love what is weakest and most confounding about ourselves, because and despite and in deference to what is essential about us.

RECENTLY, ELI AND I TOOK PENELOPE ON A WALK DOWN our street. It was a lovely Saturday afternoon in late October and as usual Eli walked ahead, kicking a stone he'd just found. Sometimes he brings along his own stone, Bessie, which he found at the beach years ago, or a branch he can drag after him. He often seeks out distractions by concentrating on several things at once, even during the most mundane activity, like watching a baseball game on TV, or taking a walk with his father before dinner. It can be annoying, as it was while walking with him, because his having to keep a step or two ahead or behind in order to keep the stone on the sidewalk made talking to him difficult. He's fourteen now and, for the most part, enjoys being complicated and different and even a little mysterious. He enjoys his obsessions with collecting and trading baseball cards and knowing everything there is to know about every automobile ever made. He gets pleasure from using the vagaries of his encyclopedic mind to research information and finding practical applications for it, like selling his cards on eBay based on which player did well the day before, or creating games out of recognizing old

Italian and French cars no one else can. He likes having a large appetite for knowledge and being a smart, odd-minded teenager whose parents are a poet and sculptor, while most of his friends' parents are in construction, real estate, and on Wall Street. He enjoys being similar and very different from me.

Like Eli, I had my obsessions—a fantasy world of comic books, movies, drawing and painting, and finally literature. I also wasn't conventional or cool in middle and high school, and I certainly knew that I was different. But Eli, through the self-knowledge and support he's received growing up knowing about his dyslexia, has the distinct advantage of liking himself. He sees these other kids as being different from *him*. Despite the difficulties his learning disability has posed, I don't think there's much he would change about himself—it would mean giving up too much. His love of platypuses, for example. He discovered the platypus when he was seven and saw a picture of one in school. We celebrated his bar mitzvah with a large white cake with a green platypus in the center; he also proudly wears a T-shirt with a drawing of a platypus that reads: "With our powers combined we are . . ." that has drawings of an alligator, a beaver, a snake, and a duck. One would be hard put to find a parent of a dyslexic child who wouldn't immediately recognize why Eli was fascinated with this semi-aquatic, venomous, fur-covered, duck-billed, beaver-tailed, otter-footed, knuckle-walking, egg-laying—one of only five—mammals. As I watched him kick his stone down the street into the brilliance of an autumn twilight, I knew that my son, like the platypus, despite everything, would not only survive the mysteries of his magical, hybrid nature, but would thrive.